THE BLUEPRINT

HOW THE HOLY SPIRIT CONNECTION CHANGED MY LIFE

Written by

Yolonda Troupe Smith

The Blueprint: How the Holy Spirit Connection Changed My Life

Published by Get Heard Publishing House, an Elevated Missions PREP, Inc. company.

Paperback: 978-1-964111-14-8

Hardcover: 978-1-964111-15-5

DEDICATION

To God,

Thank You for Your unconditional love, for having a divine plan for my life, and for every one of Your children. You are everything to everyone, and You have taken such good care of me and my family. No other god compares to You. You are amazing, holy, righteous, all-powerful, a waymaker, a miracle worker, a promise keeper, a healer, and so much more. I never want to live a single moment without You leading my life. Thank You for everything, Daddy.

To My Husband, E. Donell Smith,

Thank you for being an amazing husband. When we married, my dad said, “I don’t have to worry about you and the boys anymore because God has given you a great husband.” I believed him then, but now, after experiencing this journey with you, I know, without a doubt, that our marriage is a Holy

Spirit hookup. It is a miracle to find a husband who:

- Loves God wholeheartedly,
- Loves and supports me unconditionally,
- Loves and leads his family with wisdom, and
- Loves God's people with a servant's heart.

Through you, I have witnessed true love. Thank you, Honey.

PREFACE

A blueprint is a detailed guide or printed plan for constructing buildings. When the builder follows a blueprint, he relies on precise specifications to build a strong structure. God, our Creator, has designed a blueprint for every person's life, guiding us toward victory. The Bible lays out the blueprint. As we read Scripture, learn its teachings, and apply its lessons, we build a strong foundation for building our lives through the guidance of the Holy Spirit. Following God's blueprint ensures that we live a life of purpose, blessings, and victory.

I believe that God has a unique blueprint for each of our lives, detailing how we will connect with the Holy Spirit, or as I like to say, get the Holy Spirit hookup.

What is the blueprint?

1. Salvation

2. Baptism with water
3. Baptism with the Holy Spirit
4. Walking in His power

This book allows me to share my journey, including how I initially ignored the blueprint my parents and the Bible had laid out for me and my potential for changing lives through teaching, embracing, and activating the Holy Spirit. Because I refused to follow the right path in my young adult years, I faced unnecessary struggles and challenges, many of them self-inflicted. However, those struggles became the fuel that eventually led me to the Holy Spirit. Once I activated His power in my life, my failures became victories. Then, God prompted me to share my journey. That prompt began one Sunday morning while I sat in Sunday School listening to the teacher. By this time, I was in my forties.

As I sat in class listening to the teacher discuss the Holy Spirit and asking questions, I kept my mouth shut, hoping not to be noticed because I felt embarrassed. I did not know enough about the Holy Spirit to answer the questions confidently, and I did not want to draw attention to myself. Instead, I listened intently with the expectation that I would learn. Yet, even as I sat there, I could hear God prompting me. "You need to study."

Whoever said what you don't know won't hurt you lied. I found out firsthand that ignorance can cost you dearly. Like many believers, I accepted Jesus Christ as my personal Savior at nine years old. I was overjoyed because I had done the big one. I was walking the Christian Walk. And though salvation has remained the greatest blessing of my life, I realized something critical was missing. I did not understand the power of the Holy Spirit. Only when I began studying did I grasp what I had missed. If you had asked me to describe the Holy

Spirit back then, I would have confidently declared, "He's my Helper! He's my Comforter! He's the One Jesus left behind for me!" I thought I knew Him, yet there I was, shrinking into my church seat, unable to answer basic questions about His role in my life—one of our most precious responsibilities as Christians is to share our knowledge of God. It is our commission, and we must understand the ripple effect of sharing His Word. If we invest in one person, and they invest in another, and so on, we can change the world because the power of God's Word never ends.

My inspiration for writing this book came from my journey of getting to know and appreciate the incredible gift of the Holy Spirit. It did not happen overnight. It required continuous study and what felt like daily quizzes—challenges God allowed to push me into greater understanding and deeper faith. And yes, you will hear about some of those challenges. My goal for you as a reader is simple: I want you to go beyond the generic descriptions of the Holy Spirit and experience Him for yourself.

- When have you truly felt Him as your Comforter?
- When has He helped you in a time of need?
- Did you sense His presence when you cried those lonely tears?
- Have you ever activated His power in your life?

These were the questions I had to ask myself. Then, when I finally experienced the truth for myself, I was left with one final question: Why would anyone want to live without Him? Hosea 4:6 says, "My people are destroyed for lack of knowledge" (KJV). Again, what you don't know absolutely can hurt you.

As you dive into this book, know that I have walked the same road you are traveling now, and I am still on the journey. You will learn that when your life aligns with the Holy Spirit, your experiences exceed anything you've ever imagined. I have filled this book with powerful testimonies chronicling my experiences, intimate encounters with the Holy Spirit, moments of deliverance, miracles, and transformation. Undoubtedly, you will witness my growth, the twists, the turns, and the victories that only God could orchestrate. Through it all, I have learned one unshakable truth: I cannot live without Him. And after reading this book, I pray you will feel the same.

TABLE OF CONTENTS

INTRODUCTION

The first time I witnessed the Holy Spirit manifest in a way that was different from what I had been taught was at a Pentecostal church. This Pentecostal church invited our small church choir to participate in their annual Community Choir Day program, and we were amazed by what we saw. People were dancing, shouting, and running for the Lord. Honestly, it was scary, so foreign that I immediately rejected it. I told myself, "If it doesn't happen at my church, and if my pastor doesn't teach it, then it isn't right." To me, something was out of order.

At my church, we didn't express our praise and worship in such an extravagant way. Yet even though it felt strange and intimidating, something deep inside pulled at me. Since I was a teenager and with my friends, we sat as far back in the church as possible, which gave us a full view of eve: happening. The sanctuary held over two hundred people, and choirs filled every seat. All around me, I saw church choir robes of every color beautifully displayed throughout the pews. Each group proudly represented their home church; they had come to sing—just like we did.

This Pentecostal church's band was at the very front of the church. Not only did they have multiple instruments, but somehow, I could hear the instruments themselves praising God. I remember watching a church member expertly slide a tambourine up and down their hands, flipping it left and right while staying perfectly in sync with the beat. The drummer played the drums with such power and emotion that he seemed to shake the very foundation of every song. The organ released a sound that made me want to explode into dance, and the piano blended seamlessly, creating a joyful noise unto the Lord. Their worship was captivating, pulling everyone into God's presence. Although it was the most powerful sound, I had ever heard, we had no idea what was happening. I couldn't help but wonder, "What are they doing to make the instruments sound like that?"

Before choirs began their A & B selection rotation, they held a testimony service, another foreign concept to me. Each person stood up and started with the exact words. "I would like to give honor to God, the head of my life. I thank God that I am saved, sanctified, filled with the Holy Spirit, and baptized with the mighty burning fire." Then, with boldness and joy, they shared their testimonies, describing their struggles, breakthroughs, and victories through the aid of the Holy Spirit. Their words were on fire with praise, yet something inside of me felt conflicted. Their appearance was so different from what I was used to, and that's when I realized why we viewed Pentecostal girls at our school differently.

I assumed that they couldn't enjoy life. The girls in their church couldn't wear pants or nail polish, couldn't go to games or school events, and had church at the center of their lives—while we wanted to run from church! We laughed at their church culture, analyzed their actions, and judged their behavior as "too much"—yet here we were, singing praises to the same God. Why was that? Despite our differences, we all believed God was real, we were His children, and our worship brought us together. Though I felt God's presence in a way I had never experienced, my mind remained closed. I wasn't ready to give up my fun, fashion, or way of life. I feared that if the Holy Spirit took control, He would take away everything I enjoyed. Years later, my mindset would change completely.

As I reflected on my early encounters with the Holy Spirit, I realized:

1. I lacked knowledge and exposure, and
2. I selfishly wanted to control my own life.

The truth was that I was perfectly happy knowing just the basics—only sipping on the milk of who the Holy Spirit was. Here's all I knew at that time.

1. He descended like a dove when John the Baptist baptized Jesus. *See Matthew 3:13-17.*
2. He appeared on the Day of Pentecost as a mighty rushing wind and tongues of fire. *See Acts 2:1-4.*
3. He is part of the baptismal command. As they dip you in the water, the pastor or preacher would say, "I baptize you in the name of the

> Father, the Son, and the Holy Spirit." *See Matthew 28:19-20.*

Despite my Sunday School teacher's lessons and pastor's sermons, I wasn't paying attention. I was too busy unwrapping candy. I was too busy daydreaming. I was too busy whispering to my friends. I never studied my Bible or prepared for Sunday School—even though I knew a lesson was coming! That was the teacher's job, right? I was just there to read a verse or two and call it a day. Because of that, I couldn't see the connection between the Holy Spirit and everyday life. Despite my attitude and lack of knowledge, God was still planting seeds in me that would one day take root and shape my life.

My contentment with doing the bare minimum sustained me for a long time until life forced me to seek a deeper relationship with God. When my life took dangerous turns, I realized that only God could save me. That's when I became open to the Holy Spirit's guidance. That's when I realized I could not live without Him. If we took a quick poll, I believe many of you reading this book have had similar experiences. So many of us are Christians, yet we are living without the power the Holy Spirit has to offer. Throughout the rest of this book, I will share how the Holy Spirit showed up in my trials, tribulations, and triumphs and how you can activate His power in your life. Take a front-row seat to my journey. Learn about the person of the Holy Spirit. Gain a deeper understanding of His role in your life. See how I fully activated Him in my life. Discover how to activate Him in yours. Let's go on a journey together. Your life will never be the same.

"His presence produces life and creates life-changing experiences."

CHAPTER 1

WHO IS THE HOLY SPIRIT?

I didn't understand what the seasoned saints meant when they said, "Something got ahold of me!" until something did get ahold of me. Now, as a more mature Christian, I realize that something was the Holy Spirit. So, who is the Holy Spirit?

It was the summer of 1971, a typical hot Mississippi summer. My friends and I spent our days playing in the backyard, staying outside until the streetlights flickered on. We played hopscotch, hide-and-seek, and Red Light, Green Light, competing to see who the block champion would be. The magnolias were in full bloom, the honeysuckle was sweet. By the time I got home for dinner, my pigtails were loose, and my clothes stuck to my sweat-covered body, exhausted from running home to beat the setting sun. Often, my mom met me at the door with the threat of a whippin' for waiting until the very last minute to come inside.

Once home, I knew the routine. I would wash my hands, help Mama with anything, and prepare for our family meal. Usually, Daddy or Mama would say grace until I was old enough to pray myself— careful to remember to ask God to bless our meal, the one who prepared it, and anyone else's name we needed to lift in prayer. Through these mealtime and bedtime prayers, I first knew God existed. I remember my parents teaching me never to go to bed angry. "Come together, forgive, and then take your rest," they would say. Because of what they modeled, I never doubted that God was real. I couldn't see Him, but I knew He was there. So, each night, I would kneel by my bed, pray, and say the words my parents taught me. But on one summer day, everything changed for me in the most wonderful way.

One day, as my friends and I played, some mentioned they planned to sit on the mourner's bench to get saved. The mourner's bench was a designated row in the church for those considering becoming Christians or being born again. During revival services, those who felt ready would rise from the bench and walk to the front of the church, publicly declaring their decision to follow Christ. At the end of the revival, they would be baptized and officially recognized as Christians. But my church wasn't having a revival then; thus, I couldn't join my friends on the mourner's bench. Still, I had made up my mind. I marched home and told my parents I was ready to accept Jesus Christ as my Savior. They reached out to the church, and before I knew it, I was on my way to revival.

That week, my friends, I, and other children lined the mourner's bench, waiting expectantly for our time. Each night, we sat quietly while the guest minister delivered his sermon. Before the service, they sternly reminded us to pay close attention— no talking or moving. At home, we weren't allowed to play; instead, they told us to meditate on what we were learning. I struggled a bit with this. Sitting on the porch, I watched the other neighborhood kids playing, but I stayed put, trying to keep my mind on Jesus. In my heart, I already believed in Him. I knew Jesus existed from about the age of four—Christmas and Resurrection Sunday (Easter) programs ensured that. We sang about Him in the choir, learned about Him in Sunday School, and heard about Him in BTU (Baptist Training Union), along with countless other faith-building experiences.

By the end of the revival week, something unusual had happened—not one of us had left the mourner's bench to confess our faith. The congregation was puzzled; this had never happened before. I was caught up in the music, singing songs like *I Feel the Fire Burning in My Heart* and stomping my feet in unison with the others. But still, none of us felt the prompting to move. Now, I understand why. It's not an emotion that moves us—it's the Spirit of God.

It was Saturday, the last night of the revival. The saints had gone home and prayed, and that night, something got ahold of every child on the mourner's bench. We began to run, shout, and call on Jesus. The feeling was electrifying. Despite that momentous experience, the preacher calmed everyone and reminded us that we needed to understand what was happening before we could be declared "saved." He then asked us the three essential questions of salvation.

1. Do you believe that Jesus Christ is the Son of God?
2. Do you believe Jesus came to Earth and died for your sins?
3. Do you believe that God raised Jesus from the dead and that you are saved?

One by one, we affirmed our belief. At age nine, I was saved, but I still didn't understand "the something." My believer's journey had only begun.

I knew that God was the Creator. I knew that Jesus was His Son, who gave His life so that we could have eternal life. I had heard the Holy Spirit mentioned in church. But I didn't yet understand His role in the life of a believer. I had much growing to do before I could grasp God's plan—His "blueprint"—for us all.

The Role of the Holy Spirit within the Trinity

The Holy Spirit completes God's plan, allowing the Trinity to work in the believer's life. The Trinity is one God existing in three persons, the same God but three expressions, fulfilling His divine plan to walk with us and supply all we need to live for Him.

For there are three that bear
record in heaven, the Father,
the Word, and the Holy Ghost:
and these three are one.
1 John 5:7 KJV

God the Father is the Creator of all things.

In the beginning, God
created the heaven

and the earth.

Genesis 1:1 KJV

God the Son was given to us by the Father for salvation and to secure our eternal life.

For God so loved the
world, that he gave his
only begotten Son, that
whosoever believeth in
him should not perish,
but have everlasting life.

John 3:16 KJV

For there is one God,
and one mediator
between God and men,
the man Christ Jesus.

1 Timothy 2:5 KJV

God the Holy Spirit was given to us by the Father as the Comforter and Helper to lead us toward a victorious life.

But the Comforter, which is
the Holy Ghost, whom the
Father will send in my name,
he shall teach you all things,
and bring all things to your
remembrance, whatsoever
I have said unto you.
John 14:26 KJV

On the night of the revival, the Holy Spirit—the third person of the Trinity—moved in power, prompting us toward salvation. But to truly understand "who" He is, we must go back to the beginning and first understand the role of God the Father's divine plan.

For our recollection, we first see the Holy Spirit in Genesis 1 during the Creation Story. While verse one tells us what God did, and the first part of verse two describes the state of the Earth, the latter part of verse two reveals the presence of the Holy Spirit.

In the beginning, God created
the heaven and the earth.
And the earth was without
form, and void; and darkness
was upon the face of the deep.
And the Spirit of God moved
upon the face of the waters.
Genesis 1:1-2 KJV

Later, we see Him again in Genesis 1:26-27 when God creates mankind.

And God said, Let us make
man in our image, after our
likeness: and let them have
dominion over the fish of

the sea, and over the fowl
of the air, and over the cattle,
and over all the earth, and
over every creeping thing
that creepeth upon the earth.

So God created man in his
own image, in the image of
God created he him; male
and female created he them.
Genesis 1:26-27 KJV

In Genesis 2:7, we learn how God did it.

And the Lord God
formed man of the
dust of the ground,
and breathed into his
nostrils the breath of
life; and man became

a living soul.

Genesis 2:7 KJV

Everything God created was good—until Adam and Eve sinned. After the fall, God had to send His Son, Jesus, to be the ultimate sacrifice. *See Genisis 3.*

And walk in love, as

Christ also hath loved

us, and hath given

himself for us an

offering and a sacrifice

to God for a sweet

smelling savour.

Ephesians 5:2 KJV

But God commendeth

His love toward us, in

that, while we were yet

sinners, Christ died for us.

Romans 5:8 KJV

But this man, after he
had offered one sacrifice
for sins for ever, sat down
on the right hand of God.
Hebrews 10:12 KJV

For God so loved the
world, that he gave his
only begotten Son, that
whosoever believeth
in him should not perish,
but have everlasting life.
John 3:16 KJV

But, Jesus would not physically manifest as a human for thousands of years. Throughout the Old Testament, we see God's elect receiving power to serve in unique ways.

Then Samuel took the
Horn of oil, and anointed

him in the midst of his
brethren: and the Spirit
of the Lord came upon
David from that day forward.
1 Samuel 16:13 KJV

Then went Samson
down, and his father
and his mother, to
Timnath, and came to
The vineyards of
Timnath: and, behold,
a young lion roared
against him.

And the Spirit of the
Lord came mightily
upon him, and he rent
him as he would have
rent a kid, and he had
nothing in his hand: but

he told not his father or his
mother what he had done.
Judges 14:5-6 KJV

Then the Spirit of the
Lord came upon Jephthah,
and he passed over Gilead,
and Manasseh, and passed
over Mizpeh of Gilead,
and from Mizpeh of Gilead
he passed over unto the
children of Ammon.

So Jephthah passed over
unto the children of
Ammon to fight against
them; and the Lord
delivered them into
his hands.
Judges 11:29, 32 KJV

In the New Testament, we know the Holy Spirit came upon Mary to impregnate her with Jesus Christ. We see the Holy Spirit in action when Mary visits Elizabeth. John the Baptist leaps in the womb at the presence of Jesus in Mary's womb, and the Holy Spirit descends like a dove when John the Baptist baptizes Jesus.

Now the birth of Jesus
Christ was on this wise:
When as his mother Mary
was espoused to Joseph,
before they came together,
she was found with child
of the Holy Ghost.
Matthew 1:18 KJV

And it came to pass,
that, when Elisabeth
heard the salutation
of Mary, the babe

leaped in her womb;
and Elisabeth was filled
with the Holy Ghost:

And she spake out with a
loud voice, and said,
Blessed art thou among
women, and blessed
is the fruit of thy womb.
Luke 1:41-42 KJV

And Jesus, when he
was baptized, went up
straightway out of the
water: and, lo, the
heavens were opened
unto him, and he saw
the Spirit of God
descending like a dove,
and lighting upon him
Matthew 3:16 KJV

When the Holy Spirit appears throughout the Bible, His actions tell us and demonstrate who He is as we witness Him operate. In the beginning, He was present when God transformed the dark void Earth into a place teeming with life. He was there when man was shaped, and God breathed the breath of life into his nostrils. We also witness how He planted the seed of life into Mary's virgin womb, which turned the Word into flesh. He appeared on the day of Pentecost to empower the life of Christian believers so they could begin spreading the Word of God.

The Holy Spirit is:

1. The Promise of the Father,
2. One-third of the Trinity,
3. The Giver of Life,
4. The Sustainer of Life,
5. The Comforter, and
6. The Witness that we dwell in Him and He in us.

He:

1. Helps us pray;
2. Empowers us to witness;
3. Gives us power over the enemy;
4. Teaches, guides, and reveals things to come;
5. Brings rest, peace, and joy;
6. Opens the door to spiritual gifts; and
7. Transitions us from one phase of life to another.

His presence produces life and creates life-changing experiences. You don't want to exist—living a life disconnected from God's purpose. The enemy seeks to steal, kill, and destroy every opportunity God has set up for you. *See John 10:10.* But when you activate the Holy Spirit in your life, you move from ordinary to extraordinary walking in the fullness of God's plan.

Reflection Questions

1. Have you become a part of the family of God?
2. Do you understand the meaning of salvation?
3. How does salvation affect the life of a believer as compared to the life of an unbeliever?
4. What is the Trinity?
5. How does the Trinity work in the life of the believer?
6. Who is the Holy Spirit?
7. What tasks do the Holy Spirit perform?

CHAPTER 2

WHAT IS THE HOLY SPIRIT'S PURPOSE?

I was saved, but I started to lose myself somewhere along the way. Bluntly, I was not operating with the help of the Holy Spirit because I did not know my purpose—or His purpose in my life. As a teenager, my desire for freedom—although I already had it—outweighed everything. I wanted to do what the other teens did, or at least what I thought they were doing, because it all seemed fun. I didn't understand that when people love you, they protect you.

I grew up in a small town where entertainment for teens was limited. However, I loved dressing up, singing, dancing, and socializing whenever possible. Having the ability to do these things equated to freedom, and my love for this lifestyle consumed me. I was part of a dance troupe with my cousins, and we performed at as many hometown events as possible. Sometimes, I entered contests with a dance partner at parties—and I even won first place once.

But my freedom was limited, I thought. My parents had a rule: I could attend one event per weekend, Friday or Saturday, but not both. This rule infuriated me. I thought everyone else had more freedom than I did, which meant more fun. Unfortunately, my obsession with fun would eventually lead others into trouble.

One weekend, I invited ten to fifteen girls over for a sleepover. We had already enjoyed a fun-filled weekend—attending the school game on Friday, visiting the mall, and partying at our usual spot—but it wasn't enough for me. Two cute guys lived down the street, and I wanted my friends to meet them. So, in the middle of the night, I convinced several girls to sneak out of the house and walk down the street. I almost went with them, but at the last minute, I hesitated—fearful of what my parents would do if I got caught.

I watched as my friends slowly crawled out of bed and through the bedroom window. One by one, they carefully placed one leg over the ledge, then the other, stepping softly onto the front porch. My parents were inside, sound asleep. Then, we heard it just as they stepped off the porch onto the ground—a low growl. Then, the loud, ferocious bark came. Chaos erupted. Girls screamed and scattered in every direction, running to escape the possibility of the dog biting them. The commotion was so loud that my parents woke up. As I stood in the room before the window, I watched in horror as my friends scrambled to climb back through the window—some falling onto the porch, others grabbing anything they could to pull themselves inside. The night had turned into a disaster. And, of course, after this, the real drama began.

"What were the rules, Yolonda? What were the rules?" my parents questioned. I knew the rules. I just wanted to have fun. The next day, my parents called every girl's parents, went to their house, and personally explained the situation. I could barely show my face at school that week—people were furious with me.

As I walked down the hall, trying to get to class unnoticed—instead of my usual socializing, my classmates mocked me, mimicking my parents' words. "What were the rules, Yolonda? What were the rules?" Then, they fell to the floor laughing. At the time, I didn't realize that my friends had followed my lead. God showed me I was a leader, but I misused my influence. Instead of leading others to good, I had led them into foolishness. But even after this, I still longed for the day when I would be free from my parents' rules. And I carried that mindset into my next phase of life.

When I entered college—with no supervision—I inwardly shouted, "Free at last!" It had nothing to do with Dr. Martin Luther King Jr.'s speech. Instead of focusing on why I was in college, I ramped up my party lifestyle. I was in a new state and quickly discovered that clubs were everywhere. People stayed up all night and slept all day. I was one of them. I didn't realize I was on a downward spiral with this mindset. I took "basket weaving" and other easy courses to maintain a decent GPA. In reality, I only woke up in time to dress up, parade through the student union in my fashionable outfit of the day, and prepare for the next party. Finally, I hit a wall. My grades were terrible. I was drinking. I was constantly placing myself in dangerous situations. I was not praying. I wasn't attending church. I wasn't obeying the morals and values my parents taught me. By the end of my sophomore year's first semester, I had to return home. I didn't have enough credits even to be a sophomore. My parents decided I couldn't handle college away from home unless I were in a more structured environment.

Why do I share this? Because when you don't know your purpose—or the Holy Spirit's purpose—you will lose yourself to the world. I chose a purpose different from what God intended for me. Revisiting Genesis 1:26-27, God made us in his image with the expectation that we reflect who He is and have dominion over this world, not the world having dominion over us. We are to glorify His being. In Revelation 4:11, we learn why God created us.

Thou art worthy, O
Lord, to receive glory
and honour and power:
for thou hast created all

things, and for thy pleasure
they are and were created.
Revelation 4:11 KJV

Ephesians 1:4-6 further emphasizes that God created us for Him and that He had a plan for us all along.

According as he hath
chosen us in him before
the foundation of the
world, that we should be
holy and without blame
before him in love:

Having predestinated us
unto the adoption of
children by Jesus Christ
to himself, according to
the good pleasure
of his will,

To the praise of the glory
of his grace, wherein he
hath made us accepted
in the beloved.
Ephesians 1:4-6 KJV

Thus, our Creator determines our purpose, and when we understand this, we can begin to understand the Holy Spirit's purpose. After Adam and Eve's fall in Genesis 3, sin pursued us. Every day, we choose to allow God to prevail in our lives or let the enemy take control. But we are not alone in this fight. John 3:6 says, "That which is born of the flesh is flesh; and that which is born of the Spirit is spirit" (KJV). When you accept Jesus Christ as your Savior, the Holy Spirit, the Helper, is with you. First Corinthians 3:16 says, "Know ye not that ye are the temple of God, and that the Spirit of God dwelleth in you?" (KJV). John 14:26 says, "But the Comforter, which is the Holy Ghost, whom the Father will send in my name, he shall teach you all things, and bring all things to your remembrance, whatsoever I have said unto you" (KJV). Further, He shows you when you are right and wrong, and He builds those things in you that are Godly.

Now the works of the Flesh are manifest, which are these;

Adultery, fornication, uncleanness, lasciviousness, Idolatry, witchcraft, hatred, variance, emulations, wrath, strife, seditions, heresies,

Envyings, murders, drunkenness, revellings, and such like: of the which I tell you before, as I have also told you in time past, that they which do such things shall not inherit the kingdom of God.

But the fruit of the Spirit is love,
joy, peace, longsuffering,
gentleness, goodness, faith,

Meekness, temperance: against
such there is no law.

And they that are Christ's
have crucified the flesh
with the affections and lusts.
Galatians 5:19-24 KJV

The Holy Spirit leads and guides you in your purpose. The key is to allow him to operate in your life. I had no clue about my God-given purpose in high school and college. But God had a plan, and the Holy Spirit was my Helper through it all. When we begin to operate in our purpose, we produce good fruit, and everything we do glorifies God.

Reflection Questions

1. What is the purpose of the Holy Spirit?
2. When will the Holy Spirit become a part of our lives?
3. What are the works of the flesh, and how do they affect the believers' life?
4. What is the fruit of the Spirit, and how do they affect the believers' lives?
5. Do you know your God-given purpose? If so, what is it?

“Understanding how the Holy Spirit operates is not enough—you must activate Him in your life.”

CHAPTER 3

THE HOLY SPIRIT OPERATING IN AND THROUGH US

The Holy Spirit manifests in our lives in various ways, even when we are in the early stages of our faith—our *milk state*, as babes in Christ. He often appears as the voice that warns us when something isn't right. The Holy Spirit continuously showed up when I was pursuing a worldly lifestyle after salvation. Sometimes, I listened; other times, I did not. I got it right about fifty percent of the time—but veering into the wrong fifty percent could have easily led to tragedy, jail, serious injury, or even death.

One time, my friends and I went grocery shopping. As I browsed the aisles, I was unaware one of my friends was stuffing his coat with food. When we reached the car, he opened his jacket, and the stolen items tumbled out. My jaw dropped in shock. As he bragged about what he had done, fear gripped me. I had no part in his foolishness, yet I knew I could have gone to jail. I didn't tell him to return the stolen food, but I decided to never shop with them again, and I didn't. While I may have been innocent then, there was another situation where I was the mastermind.

While playing cards with the same group of friends, our stomachs started growling one night. "Let's order pizza!" someone suggested. But there was a problem—we had no money. That's when I came up with the idea from hell. Yes, me. I planned to order several pizzas, knowing my friends would steal them from the delivery driver when he arrived. Everyone had a role to play. The guys would wait outside while I pretended to be an innocent bystander in the lobby.

The delivery driver arrived, placed the pizzas on the counter, and turned to call me. At that moment, the guys grabbed the pizzas and sprinted out the door. The driver, baffled, turned to me and said in his slow Southern drawl, “I tell you. I ain’t never seen anybody move as fast as them boys did with that pizza. They had to be track stars! Please, take these drinks for your trouble. I’m so sorry about your pizzas.” I played my part flawlessly.

Later, as we sat around eating our stolen pizzas and drinking the sodas the driver had given me, I heard something whisper, “You are allowing the devil to speak to you and lead others into evil. You aren’t just participating. You’re orchestrating. You weren’t raised like this. You’re moving further away from your Christian Walk. You are a leader, but you’re leading in the wrong direction. If you lead, let it be God's way, not yours." Yet, I ignored it. I was having too much fun.

Another time, after a night of partying, my friends and I refused to let the night end. When the downtown clubs closed, we drove out to a "hole in the wall" run-down club deep in the woods—a place that never closed. Looking back, it sounds like the beginning of a horror movie where young girls go missing.

As I scanned the room filled with drunken strangers, my mother's words echoed in my mind. "No decent girl would be caught dead in a place like this. Nothing good happens at this time of night. People out this late are only looking for one thing." I was only interested in dancing and looking good, but none of the men cared about that. To them, any woman in that club at that hour was there for their reasons. Tired of constantly fending off their advances, I decided that night would be my last time attending an after-hours club. But my partying lifestyle? I still held onto that. I had not stepped foot in a church for eight months by then. Determined to change, I planned to attend the Resurrection Day service. But when Sunday morning arrived, I was too hungover to go. I thought I was in control of my life, but my party lifestyle controlled me.

One of the scariest moments of my life happened when I unknowingly went on a date with a rapist. It started with a phone call from an unfamiliar voice inviting me to dinner. When I went downstairs to meet him, I was captivated. He was strikingly handsome. His smile, style, and smooth conversation made me forget all my instincts. Deep down, something felt off. But I ignored it. Who forgets a face like his? Foolishly, I agreed to go on a date with the two guys. At dinner, I pushed aside any lingering doubts and enjoyed myself. But when it was time to leave, he suggested we go to another college campus to continue the fun. That's when the

Holy Spirit shouted inside me, "Don't go!" Visitation wasn't allowed on that campus, so why was he so eager to go there? Panic set in, but outwardly, I remained calm. Something told me exactly what to say.

"I need to freshen up in my room first."

They agreed, thinking I would return. But once inside my dorm, I followed the Holy Spirit's instruction—I called the front desk and told them I wasn't coming back. Days later, I saw his face in the newspaper. He was the man who had been hurting and raping girls on campus. All I could do was scream, "Thank you, Jesus!" I hadn't realized how much danger I was in. But now, I knew—that "something" warning me had been the Holy Spirit. Even now, when I reflect on these moments, I praise God. The Holy Spirit was working behind the scenes, covering, protecting, and saving my life—even when I wasn't mindful of the dangers around me. But I still needed a radical shift to surrender to Him fully. That change came when my parents made me leave that school.

My mom, a dedicated high school counselor, took immediate action. She reviewed my transcript and said, "What is this foolishness? Basket weaving? Repelling? Girl, you don't even have enough credits to be a sophomore. You're wasting our money!" When they picked me up for Christmas break, they told me, "Pack it all up. You're not coming back." Tears filled my eyes as I left behind my friends and my so-called freedom. My parents, however, were determined to save me from myself. They transferred me to a small Christian college in Mississippi, my mom's alma mater. I had two choices: 1. Stay home under their watchful eyes. 2. Try this new school and regain some semblance of independence. I chose option two.

Begrudgingly, I started my college career at this small Christian college. After two months, I made a friend from one of my classes. My parents had removed me from a self-destructive environment, but that environment was still inside of me. Not long after becoming friends with this girl, we started hanging out in cars, where they smoked weed. I felt innocent enough. I was not participating, only observing, not realizing that contact smoke can get you just as high when you're sitting in the car with all the windows rolled up. This became our daily habit until she asked me if I wanted to go home with her one weekend. "Let the fun begin!" I thought.

We left campus that Friday, with an expected return on Sunday night. When we reached the family home, her family was so friendly and welcoming, and they were invested in our goal of partying the weekend away as we were planning a good time. As I met everyone, one of her sisters stood out. This friend's mom and all her daughters were very beautiful with long flowing hair. But this one sister, the oldest, was clearly different from the rest.

It was jet black when we entered her home, although the sun was still out. When she saw us, she shouted, "Hey, what it gon' be like? We gon' party." Popping her fingers, she swayed her head and body from side to side as if she were in rhythm with music. Like her mother and sisters, she had long hair, but it was unkempt, and her eyes were dark and sunken while the rest of her face was beige. I could tell that she was very beautiful at one time, too. Obviously, she was high on something.

When she spoke again, that's when I saw her teeth. They were all rotten. I was shocked, and so many thoughts were running through my head. Something said, "Look, Yolonda; take a good long look because this will be you if you don't get off this path of life that you are living. Take a good look,

Yolonda. This is where you're headed if you don't turn your life around." That was all I needed. From that moment on, I believed that I was headed in the wrong direction, and God was warning me.

When we returned to campus, I never again talked to that girl as my friend. If I passed her on campus or in class, I would offer a quick hello and keep it moving. I felt terrible, but I did not want what happened to her sister to happen to me. I cut ties with my partying friends, joined the school choir, and started attending church again. I am so grateful that God does not give us what we deserve. Through grace and mercy, He never gave up on me. Grace, giving me what I don't deserve, and mercy, not giving me what I did deserve. God is so good.

The Holy Spirit operates in our lives more deeply as we grow spiritually. He leads us toward salvation, reminds us of who we are in Christ, and helps us produce spiritual fruit.

Ye shall know them
by their fruits.

Do men gather grapes of
thorns, or figs of thistles?"

Even so every good tree
bringeth forth good fruit;
but a corrupt tree bringeth
forth evil fruit.

A good tree cannot bring
forth evil fruit, neither
can a corrupt tree bring
forth good fruit

Every tree that bringeth not
forth good fruit is hewn down,
and cast into the fire.

Wherefore by their fruits ye

shall know them

Matthew 7:16-20 KJV

If you want to fulfill God's purpose for your life, you must experience spiritual growth and produce fruit that reflects His character.

Spiritual Growth: Fruit of the Spirit

As the believer's relationship matures in Christ, their life will begin to bear the fruit of the Spirit. God loves us so much that He wants to share His character with us. We grow and become more like God by allowing the Holy Spirit to live in us. We should draw our strength and character from our roots, the Holy Spirit, just like a tree draws strength from its roots. As a tree strengthens and grows, it produces fruit for that tree. As a believer strengthens and grows in God's knowledge, the fruit of the Spirit is produced over time. Galatians 5:22-23 lays out the fruit of the Spirit as joy, peace, longsuffering, gentleness, goodness, faith, meekness, and temperance. In *Wilmington's Guide to the Bible*, author and professor H.L. Wilmington breaks it down further to give us a clear understanding of how that fruit appears. See his list.

1. love (divine concern for others)
2. joy (inward peace and sufficiency)
3. peace (a confidence and quietness of the soul)
4. longsuffering (patience, endurance without quitting)
5. gentleness (kindness)
6. goodness (love in action)
7. faith (dependability)
8. meekness (subdued strength)
9. temperance (self-control)

(Wilmington 1981)

I remember when God reminded me that I was part of His family and should act accordingly. Despite my setbacks, I graduated from college and went on to graduate school. My parents were proud, and to celebrate my achievement, they gifted me my first designer dress. It was the "baddest" dress ever—an Albert Nipon creation in cream-colored chiffon featuring a satin collar, cuffs, waistband, and buttons that flowed down my back to the hemline, with pleats that swayed as I walked.

After graduation, I took the dress to the dry cleaners. When I got it back, it had spots. My father returned it for a second cleaning, but even more spots appeared this time. I was livid. I suspected the owner of deliberately damaging my dress, as I lived in a time when racial tensions were still high, and mistreatment of Black customers was often ignored or accepted as normal. Determined to address the situation, I went to the cleaners to confront him. I was furious, and our conversation quickly escalated into a shouting match. We squared off like gunslingers at a noonday showdown. I accused him of wrongdoing, and he remained unapologetic. Young and full of fire, I laid out exactly why I believed he had stained my dress on purpose. But who was the Christian in that situation?

I had barely stepped out of the shop when I heard the Holy Spirit say, "Yolonda, you were not raised to disrespect your elders. You are also my child, and you are called to respond to life with my character. You are to bear the fruit of the Spirit, no matter the situation. Even in difficulty, you can still respond with love and kindness. You know you have to apologize to him."

I pushed back. "Daddy," I said, (that's what I sometimes call God) "No way. He ruined my dress. He needs to apologize to me. I'm not doing it." But God kept pressing me about it. Day after day, He reminded me of what I needed to do. I refused to budge. Then, one evening, my mother and I went out to dinner, and there, sitting at a table with his wife, was the owner of the dry cleaners. I knew God had set this up. I knew what I had to do. Swallowing the hard lump in my throat, I walked toward his table.

I attempted to apologize, but before I could finish saying I'm sorry, he responded, "I am sorry." He explained that the city was experiencing water problems, and that day, several angry customers had come in to express their frustration. I had been another person adding to his burden. I realized then that not only was the situation beyond his control, but I had also contributed to his already difficult day. I apologized. As I walked away from his table, I knew God had extinguished the wrong kind of fire in me and replaced it with a valuable lesson: the importance of exercising the Fruit of the Spirit. We could have resolved the issue sooner if I had shown patience, love, and self-control. Yet, I am grateful that God allowed me to make things right and to learn how to let the Holy Spirit work through me so that I can respond to life's challenges not with my character but with the character of God.

Spiritual Growth: Baptism with the Holy Spirit

The promise of baptism with the Holy Spirit is available to every believer, but the individual must ask, yield, and receive.

And it shall come to pass
afterward, that I will pour
out my spirit upon all
flesh; and your sons and
your daughters shall
prophesy, your old men
shall dream dreams, your
young men shall see visions:

And also upon the servants
and upon the handmaids

in those days will I pour

out my spirit.

Joel 2:28-29 KJV

I indeed baptize you

With water unto

repentance: but he that

cometh after me is

mightier than I, whose

shoes I am not worthy

to bear: he shall baptize

you with the Holy

Ghost, and with fire

Matthew 3:11 KJV

God is preparing the believer for His purpose by fire, which symbolizes the purifying work of God. Being saved is one thing, but being baptized with the Holy Spirit is another. The enemy, the devil, is working harder than ever to carry out his mission, as stated in John 10:10.

The thief cometh not,
but for to steal, and to
kill, and to destroy:
I am come that they
might have life, and
that they might have
it more abundantly.
John 10:10 KJV

The thief seeks to destroy as many believers as possible, convincing them they have no power. However, we cannot combat demonic attacks or live victoriously in our personal strength. A Christian needs more of God to experience true victory, and God wants us to have everything necessary to win. When believers allow the Holy Spirit to accomplish His purpose in them, they will eventually experience baptism of the Holy Spirit, continue maturing in Christ, bear the fruit of the Spirit, and operate in their spiritual gifts. Without God's power, walking in the Spirit is impossible.

In my twenties, my desire to experience God's victorious power grew as I faced a situation I could not handle alone. One night, at the end of Bible study, the pastor asked if anyone wanted the Holy Spirit to rule and reign in their life, emphasizing that without Him, we could not live victoriously. I felt the Holy Spirit pulling me forward, so I walked to the front.

As a volunteer prayed for me, my desire for the baptism of the Holy Spirit grew stronger. But to my disappointment, there was no outward sign. I had done my part and invited the Holy Spirit to take control, so why wasn't I speaking in tongues? I didn't understand why there was no immediate evidence of this step I had taken. But God had already set the next stage of my spiritual journey in motion.

Later in my career, God assigned me to counsel a young man struggling with severe mental and spiritual issues. When we talked, he shared his experiences of devil worship, and I found myself questioning why God had placed him in my life. We had nothing in common, and our conversations terrified me.

His family moved into a neighborhood where the people openly practiced devil worship. The rituals involved skinning infants, drinking blood, and other ungodly activities. As I listened, I felt my stomach turn. When he offered to share his collection of satanic books with me, I firmly told him that God had all power in His hands and that he needed to be on the winning side. Yet, I still didn't understand why God had me listening to him.

One day, during our talks, he said, "I enjoy every conversation with you. You think you're slick. You talk about a thousand things, but before we finish, you always slip in a little Jesus." Later, he admitted that he didn't believe God was a God of love because He had taken something from him. That loss had twisted his perception of God and fueled his anger, making it easy for him to join a cult when they approached him. As he shared more, I felt utterly unequipped to handle the situation. But I held onto two scriptures that helped me stand firm despite my fear: 1 John 4:4 and 2 Timothy 1:7. First John 4:4 says, "Ye are of God, little children, and have overcome them: because greater is he that is in you, than he that is in the world" (KJV). Second Timothy 1:7 says, "For God hath not given us the spirit of fear; but of power, and of love, and of a sound mind" (KJV). I didn't let him see my fear. I straightened my back and sat up as a warrior for the King, but deep inside, I knew I was still lacking something.

One afternoon, burdened for this young man's soul, I fell to my knees and began praying for him. The thought of him spending eternity in hell devastated me. I prayed until I cried—tears that seemed endless. As the tears flowed, I kept praying. And then, suddenly, my tongue loosened, moving at lightning speed. I didn't understand the words coming out of my mouth, but I knew the Holy Spirit had consumed me. This was the moment I had been waiting for. I was filled with the Holy Spirit with the evidence of speaking in tongues. What an incredible, powerful experience! I had asked for divine help because I knew I couldn't handle this situation alone. And now, the two scriptures that had sustained me earlier became even more real. When I rose from my knees, I was transformed. I had received comfort, peace, and the strength to engage in conversations with this young man, not with fear, but with confidence that God was with me. From that moment forward, I was a powerful mouthpiece for God every time we met. Fear no longer gripped me because I knew I wasn't fighting alone. Speaking to God in prayer, naturally and spiritually (in tongues or my prayer language) became my way of building myself up to battle the enemy and win. As Jude 20 says, “But ye, beloved, building up yourselves on your most holy faith, praying in the Holy Ghost” (AKJV).

Looking back, I realize that listening to this young man’s confessions of his demonic lifestyle had scared me into the next level of God’s plan for my life. I grew spiritually through the experience. Several years later, I ran into him again. He was a completely different person. He had transformed from a bitter young man angry with God into someone who had reconnected with Him. He was proud to tell me he had finished college and began his career. With a smile, he pulled out his wallet and showed me the miniature copy of his college diploma. I was so grateful that I had taken my assignment seriously and continued meeting with him. The Holy Spirit had used me to help someone else grow spiritually—and, in turn, had allowed me to grow. I firmly believe that when I handle God’s business, He handles mine. God uses people to help people. What an incredible plan! That day, I understood something important. When I walked to the front of the church years earlier to receive the Holy Spirit, I opened the door for Him to enter my life. He had been with me from the moment I became a believer, but He was waiting for me to ignite the flame and surrender control. When I called on the Holy Spirit while praying for the young man, I stepped into God's blueprint for believers: to walk in spiritual power and impact others. Speaking in tongues is a powerful tool given to every believer to combat the enemy. It is not a one-time experience but a daily weapon to overcome the devil's tricks and traps.

Spiritual Growth: Tongues

When a person speaks a language unknown to them under the guidance of the Holy Spirit, this is speaking in tongues. It shows the Holy Spirit's ability to supernaturally and instantly give the believer the ability to communicate in a language unknown to the speaker. The experience may vary depending on the situation, but one thing remains clear: speaking in tongues is a supernatural act guided by the Holy Spirit.

Four purposes of speaking in tongues exist.

1. **We speak in tongues, so the Holy Spirit controls the whole body.** On our own, we cannot fully control how we speak. However, surrendering our tongues to the Holy Spirit and allowing Him to speak through us in an unlearned language demonstrates complete submission to God. As James 3:8 says, "But the tongue can no man tame; it is an unruly evil, full of deadly poison" (KJV).

2. **We speak in tongues as a sign.** Jesus' disciples speaking in tongues during Pentecost was the first move of the Holy

Spirit fully manifesting in the life of believers. At Pentecost, a crowd gathered after hearing a great noise. The crowd heard the disciples speaking various languages when they entered the house where the disciples were. The disciples, filled with the Holy Spirit, spoke in tongues unknown to themselves but understood by others. The Holy Spirit used the disciples' mouths to communicate in the languages of those present, allowing the crowd to hear God's message and receive the gospel. Acts 2:4 says, "And they were all filled with the Holy Ghost, and began to speak with other tongues, as the Spirit gave them utterance" (KJV). First Corinthians 14:22 says, "Wherefore tongues are for a sign, not to them that believe, but to them that believe not: but prophesying serveth not for them that believe not, but for them which believe" (KJV).

3. **We speak in tongues to speak to God.** First Corinthians 14:2 says, "For he that speaketh in an unknown tongue speaketh not unto men, but unto God: for no man understandeth him; however in the spirit he speaketh mysteries" (KJV). The Holy Spirit speaks through the believer, allowing the Spirit to take control so we can talk to God spirit to spirit because God is spirit. This form of tongues is often called a personal prayer language, used to edify the individual. God is perfect in all He does.

4. **We speak in tongues for our edification and the edification of others when a prophecy is attached.** First Corinthians 14:4 says, "He that speaketh in an unknown tongue edifieth himself, but he that prophesieth edifieth the church" (KJV). As God's children, we live in a world filled with sin, temptation, trials, and the enemy's

attacks. Our bodies and minds can be weakened and destroyed without God's guidance. Speaking in tongues builds up the believer, providing strength and spiritual fortitude, but speaking in tongues also edifies others when God reveals a specific word for those present.

According to Bishop Jerry Hutchins in his book *Understanding the Holy Spirit and the Full Gospel Baptist Church Fellowship*, there are three types of tongues (Jerry F. Hutchins 2005).

1. The speaker does not understand what language they speak, but the hearer does know because it is in the hearer's native tongue.

It is a supernatural act that allows unbelievers to receive God's message, as evidenced by the Day of Pentecost. Revisiting Acts 2, we know that the crowd gathered after hearing a great noise, and after entering the house, they could hear them speaking in various languages, specifically in the native languages of those in the crowd.

And how hear we every
man in our own tongue,
wherein we were born?

Parthians, and Medes,
and Elamites, and the
dwellers in Mesopotamia,
and in Judaea, and
Cappadocia, in
Pontus, and Asia,

Phrygia, and Pamphylia, in
Egypt, and in the parts of
Libya about Cyrene, and
strangers of Rome, Jews
and proselytes,

Cretes and Arabians, we do hear them speak in our tongues the wonderful works of God.
Acts 2:8-11 KJV

Thinking back to a personal experience, one of my son's friends who hailed from a different country visited our home. While this friend was there, I began speaking in tongues. I did not know the language, but this friend exclaimed that I was speaking their native language. This friend got saved, was baptized, and joined our family church.

2. The speaker nor the hearer understands the language, but God provides an interpreter. This happens typically during public worship when the Holy Spirit wants to deliver a message to the church. The Bible specifies how this should happen to avoid confusion or disorder.

I would that ye all spake
with tongues but rather
that ye prophesied: for
greater is he that
prophesieth than he
that speaketh with
tongues, except he
interpret, that the church
may receive edifying.

If any man speak in an
unknown tongue, let it be
by two, or at the most by
three, and that by course;
and let one interpret.

But if there be no interpreter,
let him keep silence in the
church; and let him speak
to himself, and to God.

1 Corinthians 14:5, 27-28 KJV

I attended a service at a non-denominational church where a person stood and spoke in tongues before the congregation. The room fell silent, and another individual immediately stood to interpret the message. It was incredible to witness the Holy Spirit operating in both the speaker and the interpreter, delivering a word from God to His people. I understand that it is equally important to have the gift of tongue interpretation and the gift of speaking in tongues. These gifts displayed together are a mighty move of God. God used them powerfully, and I was honored to have experienced these spiritual gifts.

3. The speaker does not understand what they are speaking, but only God does. This is sometimes called praying in the Spirit or prayer language and is intended for private worship to strengthen the believer and equip them for spiritual victory.

For he that speaketh in an
unknown tongue speaketh
not unto men, but unto God:
for no man understandeth
him; howbeit in the spirit he
speaketh mysteries.
1 Corinthians 14:2 KJV

Praying always with all prayer
and supplication in the Spirit,
and watching thereunto
with all perseverance and
supplication for all saints.
Ephesians 6:18 KJV

But ye, beloved, building up
yourselves on your most holy
faith, praying in the Holy Ghost.
Jude 1:20 KJV

I regularly experience two types of speaking in tongues: when I am around other believers who exercise their prayer language in a certain setting and when I pray in tongues alone. We are speaking to God and equipping ourselves for life. It is an amazing, powerful experience.

In my time of prayer, I have witnessed the Holy Spirit transform situations from:

1. Sick to healed,
2. Sad to joyful,
3. Burdened to free,
4. Confused to clarity,
5. Lost to directed,
6. Lacking to provide for, and
7. Powerless to powerful.

Several situations in the Bible exist where people speak in tongues publicly and privately. I have shared biblical examples and some of my own examples of the Holy Spirit and the use of tongues in the believer's life. *The Holy Spirit gives spiritual gifts to whom He chooses*, and tongues are only one of the tools that He gives to His people as He equips them for ministry. Every believer should embrace the incredible gift that Jesus left for us. When we follow His lead, the Holy Spirit empowers us to bear the fruit of the Spirit and operate in our spiritual gifts. What a victorious life!

Spiritual Growth: Spiritual Gifts

A spiritual gift is a God-given ability empowered by the Holy Spirit used for ministry to help others. The Holy Spirit grants spiritual gifts to every believer when they accept Jesus Christ as their Savior. You can't buy or work for them. These gifts glorify God, edify the believer, and strengthen the Church. A believer's service should align with the spiritual gift they have received.

The Bible outlines various spiritual gifts in Ephesians 4:7-13, Romans 12:3-8, and 1 Corinthians 12. Believers can only operate in these gifts after being baptized with the Holy Spirit. Speaking in tongues and interpreting tongues are among these gifts, but others include wisdom, knowledge, faith, healing, miracles, prophecy, and discernment of spirits.

But the manifestation of
the Spirit is given to every
man to profit withal.

For to one is provided
by the Spirit the word
of wisdom; to another
the word of knowledge
by the same Spirit;

To another faith by the
same Spirit; to another

the gifts of healing by
the same Spirit;

To another the working
of miracles; to another
prophecy; to another
discerning of spirits; to
another divers kinds
of tongues; to another the
interpretation of tongues:

But all these worketh
that one and the selfsame
Spirit, dividing to every
man severally as he will.
1 Corinthians 12:7-11 KJV

Core Spiritual Gifts

1. Wisdom: A God-given ability to resolve complex situations.

2. Knowledge: Supernatural insight into things previously unknown.
3. Faith: A divinely strengthened trust in God's power and ability.
4. Healing: A supernatural gift for bringing deliverance from diseases and infirmities.
5. Miracles: The ability to perform supernatural acts through God's power.

Additional Spiritual Gifts

1. Apostleship: The divine authority to lead, disciple, and establish churches. (1 Corinthians 12:28, Ephesians 4:11)
2. Giving: The supernatural ability to gather and share financial and material resources. (Romans 12:8)
3. Mercy: A unique ability to provide compassionate aid to those in need. (Romans 12:8)
4. Exhortation: The power to uplift, encourage, and inspire others. (Romans 12:8)

5. Ministering (Helps): The gift of assisting others spiritually and physically. (Romans 12:7, 1 Corinthians 12:28)
6. Administration: The ability to direct, organize, and oversee effectively. (Romans 12:8, 1 Corinthians 12:28)
7. Teaching: The gift of making the Word of God clear and understandable. (Romans 12:7, 1 Corinthians 12:28)
8. Evangelism: The supernatural ability to lead others to Christ. (Ephesians 4:11)
9. Tongues: Speaking in an unknown language as empowered by the Holy Spirit. (1 Corinthians 12:7-11, 14:21)
10. Prophecy: A message from God delivered through a person. (1 Corinthians 12:7-11)
11. Discernment of Spirits: The ability to distinguish between spirits from God, Satan, or man. (1 Corinthians 12:7-11)

12. Interpretation of Tongues: A supernatural ability to explain the message's meaning in a language unknown to the listener.

God has a plan for the believers, and it includes spiritual gifts. He doesn't want us to be unaware of His plan. First Timothy 4:14 says, "Neglect, not the gift that is in thee, which was given thee by prophecy, with the laying on of the hands of the presbytery" (KJV). First Corinthians 12:1 states, "Now, concerning spiritual gifts, brethren, I would not have you ignorant" (KJV).

Understanding how the Holy Spirit operates is not enough—you must activate Him in your life. The Holy Spirit convicts, empowers, and anoints believers for their divine calling. He can enable a believer to speak in tongues, but there is a difference between simply reading about the Holy Spirit and genuinely experiencing Him. Spiritual gifts equip believers for ministry, allowing them to demonstrate

God's power and fulfill His purpose. When we use the gifts given, we glorify God and live victoriously.

Reflection Questions

1. What type of fruit are you producing daily?
2. Are you displaying Godly character or your character in your life situations?
3. What does it mean to be baptized with the Holy Spirit?
4. Is baptism with the Holy Spirit for every believer?
5. What would be missing in the believer's life if they did not choose to activate God's complete plan and move forward to be baptized with the Holy Spirit?
6. What are tongues, and how are they used with the Holy Spirit?
7. What are the four purposes of tongues, and how do they benefit the believer?

8. What are the three types of tongues, and how does this affect a believer?
9. How are tongues and spiritual gifts connected?
10. What is missing in the believer's life if they do not choose to activate God's complete plan and move forward with the Holy Spirit?
11. Are you aware of God's spiritual gifts?
12. Do you understand God's plan for the believer concerning spiritual gifts?
13. Have you unwrapped your spiritual gift yet?

“When I consistently enter into God’s presence, transformation happens, and it can happen for you, too.”

CHAPTER 4

ACTIVATING THE HOLY SPIRIT BLUEPRINT IN MY LIFE

Before we go further, let's review God's plan for the believers' walk.

Step 1
Salvation/Born Again/ Spiritual Conversion

Jesus answered, Verily, verily, I say unto thee, Except a man be born of water and of the Spirit, he cannot enter into the kingdom of God.

That which is born of the flesh is 'lesh; and that which is born of the Spirit is spirit.

Marvel not that I said unto

thee, Ye must be born again.

John 3:5-7 KJV

Man is born of water (when his mother gave birth), and man is born of the spirit (when man becomes a child of God). Romans 10:9 says, "That if thou shalt confess with thy mouth the Lord Jesus, and shalt believe in thine heart that God hath raised him from the dead, thou shalt be saved" (KJV). Thus, to claim your salvation, you must (1) confess with your mouth, (2) believe in your heart, and (3) know that Jesus died on the cross and rose from the dead. The fourth aspect of this comes after confession and belief, which is that the Holy Spirit dwells within you upon your spiritual conversion.

While we desire that everyone reading this book has already confessed their hope and faith in the Lord Jesus, I would be remiss not to acknowledge that some may not have taken this crucial first step. Therefore, if you are not saved but are ready to become a part of God's family, proceed by telling your pastor, confessing your hope and faith, and joining the church. If you prefer to start the journey now, see the following sample prayer to guide you.

Father, in the name of Jesus,
I come to you as a sinner
asking for forgiveness of my
sins. I believe that Jesus hung
on the cross, died, was buried,
and rose again. He took my
sins, and in exchange, I
received the righteousness of
God in Him. In Jesus name,
I pray. Amen.

If you prayed this prayer, I thank Jesus. You are saved and have become a part of God's family.

Step 2
Baptism with Water

When baptized by water, believers demonstrate Jesus' death and resurrection. Just as Jesus took on our sins, died, and resurrected to give us new life, going down into the water symbolizes dying to the sinful lifestyle, while coming out of the water symbolizes embracing a new life in Christ.

Know ye not, that so many
of us as were baptized into
Jesus Christ were baptized
into his death?

Therefore we are buried with
him by baptism into death:
that like as Christ was raised
up from the dead by the glory

of the Father, even so we also
should walk in newness of life.
Romans 6:3-4 KJV

Some Christians stop here and never fully live in the plan for the believer. More is available, so don't stop here. Keep moving in God's plan for your life.

Step 3
Baptism with the Holy Spirit

Have you asked for the baptism of the Holy Spirit yet? Matthew 7:11 says, "If ye then, being evil, know how to give good gifts unto your children, how much more shall your Father which is in heaven give good things to them that ask him" (KJV)? The Holy Spirit is a good gift from the Father which empowers our journey. If you have not asked for and received the baptism of the Holy Spirit, here is a sample prayer you can say.

Father, in the name of Jesus,

Forgive me for everything I have done wrong, those I know about and those I don't. Have mercy on me and hear my prayer. I desire to give up my will for your will in my life. Baptize me with the Holy Spirit so I can walk in the full plan you have created for every man.

Holy Spirit, lead me, teach me, tell me things to come, bring things to my remembrance, and be my comforter, helper, and everything you said you would be to the believer. Teach and help me bear the fruit of the Spirit in my character and operate in every spiritual gift you have given me. I receive everything that you have predestined and ordained for me.

Strengthen me and take care of me.
I am your child, and I will trust you
for all the days of my life. Thank you
for transforming me from powerless
to powerful. In Jesus name, I pray.
Amen.

Step 4
Walking in Power

Acts 1:8 says, "But ye shall receive power, after that the Holy Ghost is come upon you: and ye shall be witnesses unto me both in Jerusalem, and in all Judaea, and in Samaria, and unto the uttermost part of the earth" (KJV). This is how you live your best life. You believe. You decide to follow God's plan. You walk in the Spirit. You refuel repeatedly and get empowered to stay empowered.

God's plan for man is amazing, and when we implement his plan instead of our plan, we experience divine intervention. Who doesn't want the Holy Spirit helping in their life? I sure did and still do, but I had to learn how to activate Him.

When I was struggling in my first marriage, the stress took a physical toll on me. My hair began falling out, and I lost so much weight that I dropped from a size six to below a size two. I even had to shop in the children's section of department stores to find clothes that fit. I felt like I was losing my mind. The devil was trying to destroy me—if not physically, then certainly mentally and spiritually. He had stolen my joy and was determined to break me. But what the enemy meant for harm, God used for good, pushing me further into my Holy Spirit journey.

I met my now ex-husband through a close friend. I loved spending time with him, but one issue continuously weighed on my heart—he had not accepted Jesus Christ as his personal Savior. I knew what the Bible said about unequally yoked relationships. According to 2 Corinthians 6:14, "Be ye not unequally yoked together with unbelievers: for what fellowship hath righteousness with unrighteousness? and what communion hath light with darkness" (KJV)? Yet, I convinced myself that I could draw him to Christ, holding onto 1 Corinthians 7:14, which says, "For the unbelieving husband is sanctified by the wife, and the unbelieving wife is sanctified by the husband: else were your children unclean; but now are they holy" (KJV). Instead, I went against my better judgment—and fell into darkness. Within a year, I was involved in premarital sex and desperately asked God to allow me to marry this man. My life was a mess. I knew better, yet I still tried to negotiate with God. The Holy Spirit nudged me, my parents voiced concerns about our different spiritual foundations, and even when I sought godly counsel, I was reminded of 2 Corinthians 6:14. But I refused to listen. I told myself that marriage would somehow make everything right—that it would "fix" the sin and set things in order. Eventually, he agreed to marry me and even took steps toward salvation before our wedding. But despite our efforts, we remained unequally yoked.

Seventeen years later, I found myself packing up my two children and moving back home to my parents, exhausted, broken, and desperate for help. As I did, you can know the Word and think you are strong enough, but if you do not activate the Holy Spirit, the enemy will take full advantage of your weakness. Although my marriage was difficult, it drew me closer to God. "But as for you, ye thought evil against me; but God meant it unto good, to bring to pass, as it is this day, to save much people alive" (Genesis 50:20 KJV). This was the moment I had to learn to activate the Holy Spirit—if I hadn't, I am confident my fate would have been far worse.

I began reading the Bible daily, immersing myself in God's Word, and growing in my faith. This strengthened my desire to walk, talk, think, and act like Jesus. I spent my free time soaking in the Word through television and online sermons, watching teachers like Frederick K. C. Price, T. D. Jakes, Joyce Meyer, Clarence McClendon, and Creflo Dollar. Through this process, I rediscovered myself. I was no longer just hearing the Word; I was also believing it, obeying it, praying it, and activating it in my life. Even so, I knew I needed spiritual leadership. Finally, God connected me with a church where the pastor helped me understand scripture in a new way, allowing me to apply it to my everyday life. As a result of this immersion, I became more sensitive to hearing the Holy Spirit speak to me. Here are some ways I experienced the power of activating the Holy Spirit in my daily life.

The Pillow Shams

This situation may seem insignificant to some, but as you've seen throughout my life stories, small actions reveal who we are and who we are becoming.

I bought a twin bed-in-a-bag set, and when I opened it at home, I found two extra pillow shams inside. It was perfect—I had envisioned precisely how I wanted my bed to look and needed extra pillow shams to complete the design. My initial thought? "Their loss, my gain." I had gotten what I wanted without spending an extra dime, but by this point in my spiritual journey, I knew God wouldn't let me feel at peace about it.

A few days passed, and every time I was alone—driving, cleaning, or simply sitting silently—I heard the Holy Spirit whisper, "Pillow sham. Pillow sham. Pillow sham. Yolonda, you feel good about those extra pillow shams, but someone else is missing two pillow shams because of you. Take them back so the store can correct the mistake." I kept brushing it off, but the voice grew louder and more persistent. Finally, I couldn't take it anymore. I grabbed the two extra pillow shams and went back to the store.

I found a salesperson and explained that my bed-in-a-bag came with two extra pillow shams. I admitted that I wanted them but knew I needed to return them. To my surprise, she smiled and said, "You know what? Keep them. You took the time to bring them back when you didn't have to. Enjoy them." At that moment, I received a valuable lesson: when you obey the Holy Spirit, God will give you the desires of your heart—in His time and His way. I took the pillow shams home, inserted the pillows, fluffed them up, and placed them on my bed. Every time I looked at them, they reminded me to trust in God's timing rather than take matters into my own hands. Psalm 37:4 says, “Delight thyself also in the Lord: and he shall give thee the desires of thine heart” (KJV). Hebrews 11:6 says, "But without faith it is impossible to please him: for he that cometh to God must believe that he is, and that he is a rewarder of them that diligently seek him" (KJV). When we choose obedience, God blesses us exceedingly beyond what we could imagine.

The Money Pouch

One Sunday, I went shopping with a small pouch containing my signed income tax check, a deposit slip, and some cash. Don’t ever do this! As I was getting ready for work the following day, I realized the pouch was missing. Panic set in. I rushed to the mall parking lot, searching everywhere. I checked the ground and the garbage cans—nothing. It was too early for the mall to open, so I had no choice but to continue my day. But the thought of my signed check and hundreds of dollars missing overwhelmed me with fear. As I drove to work, I heard the Holy Spirit say, "Why don't you apply what you've been learning in church?" That's when I remembered the following verses.

And in that day ye shall
ask me nothing.
Verily, verily, I say unto you,
Whatsoever ye shall ask
the Father in my name, he
will give it you.

Hitherto have ye asked
nothing in my name:
ask, and ye shall receive,
that your joy may be full.
John 16:23-24 KJV

Confidence flooded my heart at that moment—I knew God's Word was true. Thus, I decided to put my faith into action. I prayed and asked the Holy Spirit to help me recover my pouch. When I arrived at work, my fear had lifted and was replaced with unshakable joy. I stood on God's promise. I boldly prayed that my pouch would be returned with *every red cent* and my check untouched. Then, I took the next step—I praised God in advance for my blessing. I told my coworkers what had happened when I got to the office. I declared, "I lost my pouch, but I believe God will bring it back to me."

One coworker scoffed, "You're crazy if you think you're getting that back."

Another said, "Girl, whoever found that pouch is already working with someone at the bank to cash that check."

Immediately, my praise stopped. Doubt flooded in. Maybe they're right. What was I thinking? I said out loud, "Yeah, you're right. I don't know why I thought I'd get it back with the money still inside." But thank God that wasn't the end of my story. At that moment, the Holy Spirit activated and reminded me of my pastor's sermon. He had said, "'Guard your hearing and eye gates because what you see and hear affects your faith.'" Suddenly, I realized what had happened. I had allowed the negativity to shake my faith. I repented. I asked God to forgive me for doubting. Then, I started over—praying, believing, and standing on His promise. This time, I didn't let doubt creep back in. Every day, I thanked God for bringing the pouch back untouched. Whenever I felt worry creeping in, I shut it down with praise.

For verily I say unto you,
That whosoever shall say
unto this mountain,
Be thou removed, and
be thou cast into the sea;
and shall not doubt in his

heart, but shall believe that
those things which he saith
shall come to pass; he shall
have whatsoever he saith.

Therefore I say unto you,
What things soever ye desire,
when ye pray, believe that ye
receive them, and ye
shall have them.
Mark 11:23-24 KJV

Two days later, I came home from work and found a message on my answering machine. “Please go to the McRae’s Department Store Information Desk. They have your pouch.” I shouted joyfully! But when I arrived at the store, the employee at the information desk said, “I don’t have a pouch.” Immediately, doubt crept in. Was someone playing games with me? I left the store feeling a little discouraged. A few days later, a friend who worked at McRae's called. I asked her if she could look for information about my lost pouch. She got back to me and said, "A young lady has your pouch, but she kept it in the department where she works."

The next day, I returned to the store. When I told the employee my name, she smiled and handed me my pouch. And guess what? The check and *every red cent* were still inside—just as I had prayed! It was a miracle! In times like these, when honest people are hard to find, God used someone to answer my prayer.

Ah Lord God! behold, thou
hast made the heaven and
the earth by thy great power
and stretched out arm, and
there is nothing too
hard for thee.
Jeremiah 32:17 KJV

Miracles still happen! I asked the woman if there was anything I could do to thank her for her kindness. She replied, "Nothing at all." I desired to bless her and told her I made flower arrangements and wreaths. She said she would love a wreath, so I made her the most beautiful wreath I had ever crafted—and she loved it. This experience taught me a valuable lesson. God moves when you apply what you've learned in church to your life. The Holy Spirit had worked behind the scenes in both situations, teaching me to trust Him fully.

How to Get the Holy Spirit Hookup Daily

Many ways exist to connect with the Holy Spirit, and you have to discover how you best connect with Him. However, if you want a guide, I have provided how I start my day to connect. Activating the Holy Spirit at the start of each day is essential. Yet, you should pray to confirm which times are best for you. Here is how I do it.

1. I go to my prayer spot, a dedicated space to focus on God.
2. I invite the Holy Spirit to commune with me by asking Him to take control and guide me. Here is a sample prayer.

Father, in the name of Jesus,
I invite the Holy Spirit, to fill
me and take control of my life.
I want You to perform every
work that You have ordained
for me and have Your way in
my life. I lay every gift, talent,
dream, mind, will, emotion,
spirit, body, imagination, intellect,
concern, and trust in Your hands.
I declare and decree that I operate
with the mind of Christ and the

wisdom, knowledge, and understanding of God. Cover me with the blood of Jesus. No weapon formed against me or my household shall prosper. Instruct me, teach me, and guide me with your eye. I will walk in my destiny, fulfill my purpose, and reach the destination You have for me. In Jesus' name, Amen.

3. I pray in the Spirit, allowing the Holy Spirit to control my tongue and speak through me.
4. I pray in the natural. I personalize the Lord's prayer, thank God for what He has done, and take all my concerns to Him.
5. I read the Word of God and study scriptures using a daily devotional. Also, "Read the Bible in a Year" plans have been helpful. I have seen them online and in Christian bookstores.

6. I meditate on the Word of God, spending time in God's presence while playing soft worship music to set the atmosphere.
7. I sit quietly and listen. I tell the Holy Spirit I am reporting for duty and let Him minister.
8. I journal what the Holy Spirit reveals. I write down what He speaks to my heart.
9. I obey his instructions throughout the day. When the Holy Spirit prompts me, I respond in obedience.

When I consistently enter into God's presence, transformation happens, and it can happen for you, too.

1. If I enter prayer wounded, I come out as a warrior.
2. If I enter prayer as a victim, I come out as a victor.
3. If I enter prayer sick, I come out healed.

4. If I enter prayer discouraged, I come out encouraged.
5. If I enter prayer with a mess, I come out with a miracle.

I know the Holy Spirit is my helper, and He fixes things for me. As He has done for me, He can do for you. I always tell people, “Don’t live without Him, His presence, or His works!” As I continued to activate the Holy Spirit’s blueprint in my life, I became more mature in my responses to life’s challenges.

Another Chance

While I was growing spiritually and learning how to activate the Holy Spirit in my daily life, I was losing in my marriage. Eventually, my marriage ended in divorce, and the Holy Spirit led me back home to my parents to start over. I felt like a failure. But being home allowed God to take care of me and my children. I felt depressed and shame, but hope and faith remained on the horizon. The Holy Spirit reminded me of God's promises.

O Lord my God, I
cried unto thee, and
thou hast healed me.

O Lord, thou hast
brought up my soul
from the grave: thou
hast kept me alive,
that I should not
go down to the pit.
Psalm 30:2-3 KJV

These experiences weren't just about pillow shams or a lost pouch; they were spiritual lessons.

1. The Pillow Sham situation taught me to humble myself and obey God. Whatever we desire that is good, God will provide in His time.
2. The Money Pouch situation taught me to guard my mind against negativity. I had to stay focused on God's promises and not be persuaded by doubt—otherwise, I could miss out on my blessings.

God indeed heard my cry, restored me, and gave me another chance to walk in my God-given destiny according to His blueprint. I am thoroughly convinced that you can call on the Holy Spirit and get results by:

1. Trusting in the process of prayer,
2. Reading God's Word,
3. Listening to His voice, and
4. Obeying His guidance.

I clung to one of my favorite scriptures. Jeremiah 29:11 says, "For I know the thoughts that I think toward you, saith the Lord, thoughts of peace, and not of evil, to give you an expected end" (KJV). God had a plan for me, and I wanted it. It was time to step into the next phase of my journey—continuing to follow God's plan or blueprint.

Reflection Questions

2. How many steps are in God's plan for the believer?
3. What step are you currently in during your Christian Walk?
4. Are you ready to go further in your walk if you have not completed the process yet?
5. Do you have plans for how you will go forward?

“Everyone wins when they allow the Holy Spirit to lead."

CHAPTER 5
A NEW BEGINNING

God desires to give us an expected end—a hope-filled future. While home after my divorce, I reconnected with a childhood friend. Both of us had gone through difficult marriages that ultimately ended in divorce. As we sought the Lord for direction in our lives, the Holy Spirit rekindled our friendship and ignited a romance between us. In obedience to God, we followed the path He laid before us. As we did, His blessings overflowed into our lives, and we were married. At the time of writing this book, we have been married for almost fifteen years. I gained two more children through this union, a son and a daughter. Our daughter and her husband have blessed us with two amazing grandsons. My two sons from my first marriage have grown up and begun their journeys. My oldest son is now married, and he and his wife have blessed us with our first granddaughter. Together, my husband and I have four children and three grandchildren. I am amazed by how God has blessed me in marriage, ministry, and music. I am living in the divine setup He always intended for me. However, that doesn't mean it has been without challenges. Challenges will come when you walk in the life God has called you to. As I've shared before, the enemy still seeks to kill, steal, and destroy, especially when you are an example of what God has ordained.

When we first moved to Atlanta, I faced a significant adjustment. My husband, being a pilot, needed to live in a larger city. But I was a small-town girl, and life in a fast-paced environment was overwhelming. However, the Holy Spirit provided opportunities to help me adapt. Since I was now a stay-at-home mom, I had time to volunteer at my child's school. I attended every class trip and school event, ensuring I was present for every opportunity that mattered. Over time, the Holy Spirit helped me overcome my fears of living in a big city. One of my son's passions was debate, and his competitions required travel to different parts of Atlanta. Stepping out on faith, I became more comfortable navigating the city while supporting him. Eventually, I became the go-to volunteer at my children's school.

Any time they needed extra hands, they could call on me. This opened doors for me, leading to full-time employment. I went from volunteering to holding multiple roles, from after-school theater teacher assistant to after-school theater soloist music trainer, Extracurricular Classes Department Head to school counselor, and Crew Director. The Holy Spirit guided me in each step, positioning me to serve my family while allowing me to grow professionally in ways that aligned with my desires. One of my most memorable experiences at the school was starting a club called "Gifted Hands."

A church festival inspired me to create Gifted Hands. At the festival, I saw beautiful, handcrafted quilts. The woman at the booth was from Gee's Bend, Alabama—a historic quilting community whose artwork has been displayed in over thirty major art museums nationwide. I wanted my students to experience this piece of history firsthand. At first, the students were uninterested in learning about quilting. But that changed when they discovered that many Gee's Bend quilters had been featured on Oprah Winfrey's show. Suddenly, their excitement grew, and I watched as the Holy Spirit transformed the classroom. The students learned valuable lessons from the class activities, which became valuable lessons for life. God is amazing. This experience reinforced a powerful truth: When you follow the Holy Spirit's lead, He positions you for more incredible things. By allowing God to use me in this school, I formed invaluable relationships, opening doors to more opportunities aligned with my true passions.

One of my prayers to God had been to have a worldwide ministry. I only wanted to work for Him. God heard me. After a brief illness, He transitioned me from working at the school to full-time ministry and entrepreneurship. While waiting for God to manifest the worldwide ministry fully, I began writing jingles. I wrote two jingles for the school where I worked and jingles for Bishop Paul Morton, a celebrity chef, and many others. Each jingle was created through a divine vision from the Holy Spirit. Every morning, I would wake up and ask the Holy Spirit what tasks to focus on. Each act of obedience brought me one step closer to my desires. Then, the Holy Spirit led me to my next assignment, recording a gospel album.

I prayed over every song I planned to include, humming melodies and writing lyrics, using my phone's recording system to capture ideas. As I meditated on the album, the Holy Spirit guided me to specific scriptures to incorporate into the songs. There were difficult moments when I had to push myself to keep going, but God continued to surprise me along the way. On my first album, I had the opportunity to work with a Grammy-nominated producer. I was excited to see how the Holy Spirit would orchestrate my second project. I surrendered my heart, hands, voice, and mind to the Holy Spirit. When I needed resources or connections to complete the album, the Holy Spirit stepped in and provided. One day, a bishop I met at church complimented me on how I ministered through singing. My husband, recognizing an opportunity, told him about my project. At that time, I had exhausted all of my resources. I had given everything I could to the album, but it was still missing something. When Bishop Clayton Johnson listened to my music, he said, "Your songs are good, but they could be greater with the right ingredients." Then, he connected me with a Grammy-nominated producer and other professional musicians to help complete the album.

Finishing the project wasn't easy. I traveled between two states, juggling prayers, recording sessions, and video shoots. But I kept following the Holy Spirit's lead. When He finally said, "It is complete," I was in awe of what we had

God Is.

01. God Is
02. About My Father's Business
03. Great Day Ft. Bishop Clayton "Miracleman" Johnson
04. Holy Spirit
05. Been Mighty Good
06. My Everything
07. My Everything Reprise
08. At The Altar
09. You Are My God
10. Breakloose

---

*"I know you heard the hit song from The Anointed Captivating Voice of Yolonda Troupe Smith, **Breakloose**. Well, she warned us. Now, you are really going to Break Loose with the rest of this amazing project. Every Song is uplifting and anointed. If you love Traditional, Contemporary, or Worship Music, this is the whole package. This Project is what we really need in this season. Get ready for **God Is**"*

- Bishop Paul S. Morton

produced. Once again, the Holy Spirit had proven that He was behind the scenes, shaping my destiny. With the album completed, God opened the door to my next assignment.

My husband and I began traveling for ministry with Bishop Johnson. We worked locally but also took our ministry on the road—visiting places like Germany, St. Kitts & Nevis, Trinidad, New York, New Orleans, Florida, Mississippi, Alabama, Australia, Costa Rica, Texas, Africa, Chicago, California, and North Carolina. Then, an opportunity arose to co-host a TV show. The first offer I received was for a different television show, but the Holy Spirit said, "No." But later, He said "Yes" to another opportunity—co-hosting the "Ignite Your Purpose" show on the Preach the Word Network. The Holy Spirit confirmed His presence in the show's creator, and I knew this

PREACH THE WORD
WORLDWIDE NETWORK
Ignite
Into Your Purpose
Hosts Patricia Thompson and Yolonda Troupe Smith
Every Monday at 4:30 PM Est and Pst
For On Demand and Live TV Distribuiton
visit www.ptwwntv.com

was a divine setup. Every episode featured powerful testimonies of how God transformed lives when people allowed the Holy Spirit to take control and push them into their purpose.

The lesson was clear: Everyone wins when they allow the Holy Spirit to lead. My life was changing in extraordinary ways, and I loved every minute.

But as it is written,
Eye hath not seen,
nor ear heard,
neither have entered
into the heart of man,
the things which God
hath prepared for
them that love him.
1 Corinthians 2:9 KJV

As my husband and I followed the Holy Spirit, blessings overflowed. Then came the pause. My parents needed care. Later, an aunt who had no children also needed support. I was blessed to be in a position where I could help them. But as I cared for my mother, a concern settled in my heart: "God, I haven't produced any ministry work in a while." Then, the Holy Spirit gave me an assignment. He instructed me to record a Christmas song—but not alone. He specifically told me to sing a duet with another woman. We met via Zoom half the time while I continued caring for my mom. I didn't know how God would do it, but I walked by faith, and we finished the song. Shortly after, my mother transitioned.

After my mother's passing, grief weighed heavily on me. I had no desire to do anything except rest. But in my grief, the Holy Spirit whispered, "Release the Christmas song." I obeyed. Even in my season of mourning, God used that song. Each

Yolonda Troupe Smith
Just For Me
FT. LARONDA DAWSON

Just For Me
FT. LARHONDA DAWSON
PRODUCER
Xavier "Professor X" Fairley
(recorded in X-Factor Studios)
Atlanta, GA
BACKGROUND VOCALS
Ebony Rose Green-Capers, Angelique Sally, Solomon Capers
MUSIC PRODUCTION
Solomon Capers - Piano
Xavier Fairley - Drums
Stello Clark - Bass & Guitar
VOCAL & MUSICAL ARRANGEMENT
Xavier Fairley
(X-Factor Studios),
Yolonda Troupe Smith
MIXING AND MASTERING
Etienne "EJ" Porter
(Drummerboy Entertainment
& Recording Studios)
Sarasota, FL

year, it has done well. The Holy Spirit guided me through every step—music ministry, word ministry, family, travel, and even grief. What seemed like detours were God-ordained pauses for me to care for the family while still walking in my calling.

What did I learn? Obedience to the Holy Spirit will always lead to victory. My father was gone. My mother was gone. My aunt was gone, and a new year had come. I had cared for my loved ones for ten years, but now it was time to wake up and step into the next season of my life. My last child was finishing college, and life was transitioning again. I reflected on future ministry goals, helped my husband with his business, worked in my local church, and resumed traveling with Bishop Johnson. I preached, sang, wrote songs, and served in any capacity the Holy Spirit led me. I was moving forward. Then, one day, while on a walk with my husband, I fell—and life transitioned again. For forty-five minutes, I lay on the ground in excruciating pain. My husband and I were walking our son's dog when two other dogs came running toward us. My husband was a few steps ahead with our son's dog while I instinctively positioned myself to stop the dogs. But as they rushed toward me, I started to fall. I tried to catch myself, but instead, I hit the ground with my arms outstretched—and two broken bones pierced through my skin. I was rushed to the hospital for emergency surgery and spent several days there before they cast my arm. We needed help, so we enlisted my cousin and a close friend to assist us during my recovery. Yet, while I was recovering, I noticed a foul smell coming from my arm during the healing process. I went to an urgent care facility; the doctors removed my cast—and what I saw was horrifying. My arm was covered in large black blisters. I had developed an extremely rare pain syndrome in my hand that affects only five percent of patients. None of the doctors had ever seen anything like it. After several consultations, a kind dermatologist finally gave us an answer. I had

Bullae fracture blisters (bullae)— a condition so rare that it hadn't been documented in over 100 years (figure of speech). I knew this was a spiritual attack—the enemy was trying to stop my ministry.

Recovery at home was brutal. My wound had to be cleaned and rebandaged twice a day. I was in constant pain. I had to sleep in a recliner for nine months. I was still grieving my mother's passing. I found myself asking God why. At the same time, I refused to stay in a sleep-induced, medicated state. With my husband's help, I got rid of every addictive prescribed drug and clung to God's promise that the Holy Spirit would carry me through this ordeal. Following my doctor's instructions, I always kept my arm elevated with three pillows—no matter where I traveled. My husband took six weeks off work to care for me. My cousin stayed for one week. My girlfriend stayed for two weeks. A nurse came once a day to change my bandages. Eventually, I had to learn to change my bandages once a day by myself when my cousin and friend left. I was frustrated. When the doctor finally cut my stitches, after waiting for the blisters to heal, the wounds reopened where the bones had initially broken through. I needed help but didn't trust my children to have the skills to assist me. So, I did what I knew best. I prayed. The Holy Spirit showed me how to turn my arm so the bandage would stay in place. Even though I followed His instructions, I still struggled. I felt ashamed of how deformed my hand and arm looked. Depression started to creep in. Then, one day, Bishop Johnson called. "Elder, what's going on?"

I listed every problem I faced and ended with: "I'm just going to stay away from people and only go to my doctor's appointments."

His response shook me awake: "Fight, Elder! Get back to working for God. You can't let the devil steal your life."

I turned to God. “Lord, what is going on?” Then, I heard one phrase replaying in slow motion: “Donell, I am falling.” I started researching why people hear or see things in slow motion during accidents—and I discovered something remarkable: I had time to change my outcome. God spoke clearly.

“When you were falling, you had time to call on Me. You could have said cover me, protect me, but instead, you called out to your husband. He loves you, but He doesn’t have all power in his hands. He is not in control. I am. You must learn to speak the right words in all situations. Wherever you go, the enemy will try to attack, but you must speak, believe, and activate My Word to destroy him. Tell My people to stay connected to the Holy Spirit and declare My Word so they receive divine intervention in every area of their lives. Do not sit back and let the devil do whatever he wants.”

God's Word reminded me of Philippians 4:6, "Be careful for nothing; but in every thing by prayer and supplication with thanksgiving let your requests be made known unto God" (KJV). We must fight when we face sickness, financial struggles, and family issues. Speak God's Word, believe in His promises, and activate His power. As Matthew 11:12 reminds us, "And from the days of John the Baptist until now the kingdom of heaven suffereth violence, and the violent take it by force" (KJV). As Bishop Johnson said, "'What are you going to do when you are attacked?'" Fight! Take it by force! Use your faith in God and His Word. Step by step, I took it by force.

1. I prayed for healing, guidance, and strength.
2. I poured my heart out to God.
3. I read the Word daily.
4. I cleaned my wound faithfully.

Left Forearm Front View

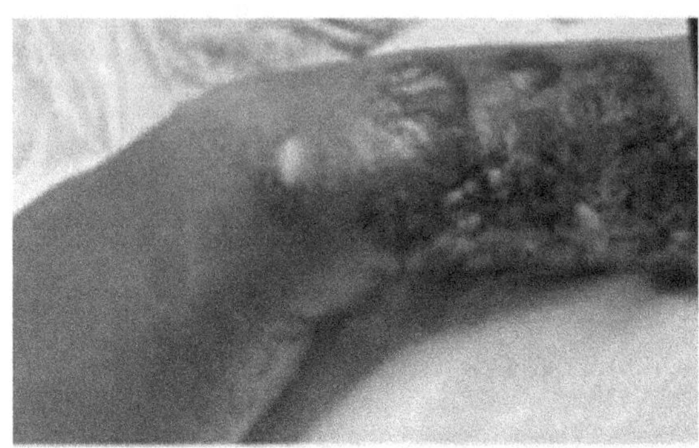

Before

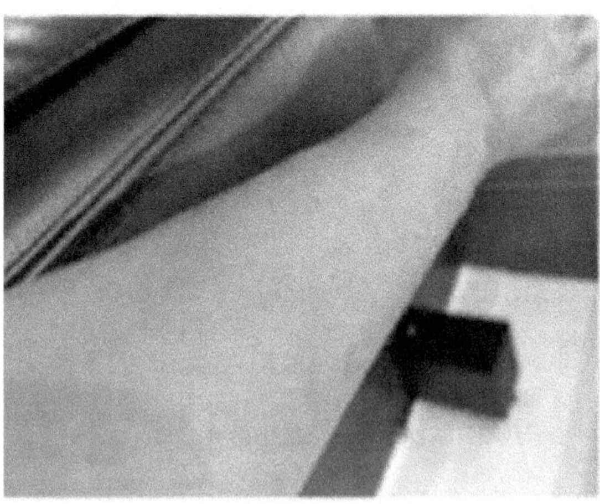

After

Left Forearm Back View

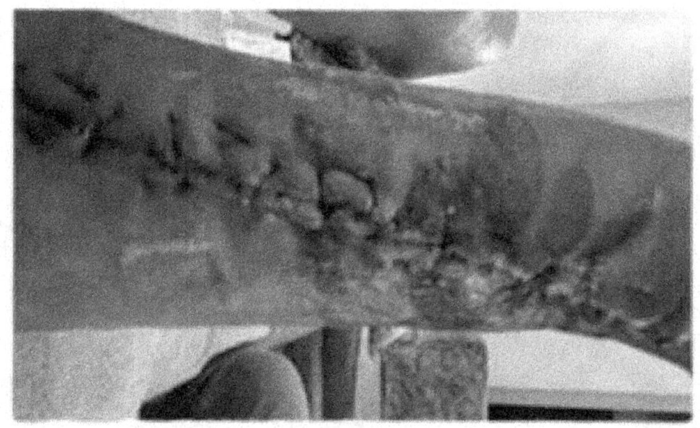

Before

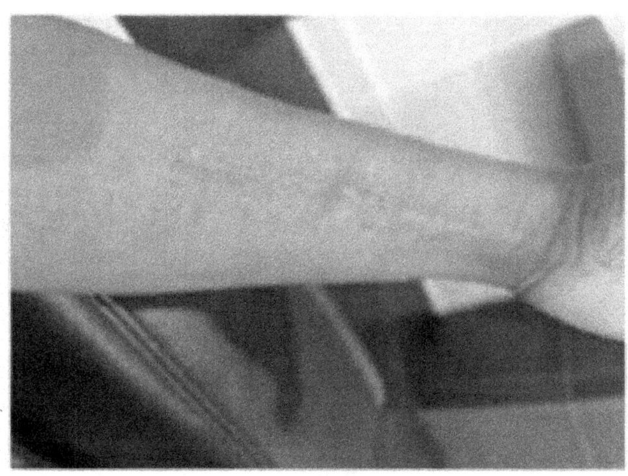

After

Left Forearm Side View

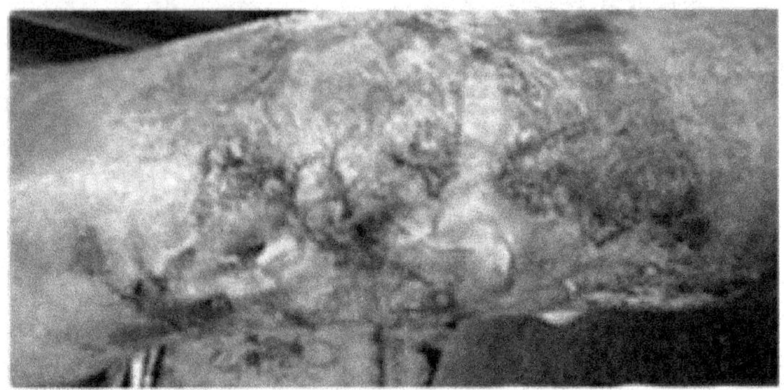

Before

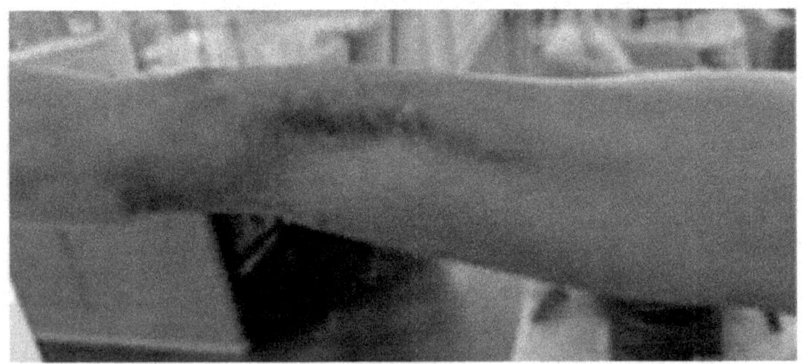

After

5. I exercised despite the pain.
6. I followed the doctor's plan.
7. I spoke God's promises out loud.
8. I thanked God in advance.
9. I shared my testimony of God's works.

God allowed me to overcome by activating the Holy Spirit, and I got out of the recliner, out of the house, and back to ministry. Seventeen months of physical therapy was painful and challenging, but I give all the glory to God. Through it all, God remained faithful.

Today, my family and I are excited about the new home God has blessed us with—a place of peace and restoration. We plan to fish in the lake; enjoy coffee, tea, and lemonade on the deck; and cherish our time with our grandchildren, teaching them to swim. Most importantly, we share our faith with them—

passing down the wisdom of trusting God's blueprint.

God never left me through every challenge—grief, pain, and hardship. He still speaks. He still heals. He still restores. And through it all, I continue to live for Him.

CONCLUSION

God has given us the blueprint for a victorious life. To walk in this victory, we must:

1. Know who the Holy Spirit is,
2. Understand His purpose,
3. Learn how He operates, and
4. Activate His power in our lives.

This is what I call getting the Holy Spirit hookup. As I conclude, I want you to take away one powerful truth: God is waiting for you. The Holy Spirit is already present, ready to lead and empower you. Once you confess Jesus as Lord and Savior and are baptized as a symbol of your newness, God begins the process of your spiritual maturation. Spiritual growth mirrors natural growth—from infancy to toddlerhood and adolescence to spiritual maturity. Living a saved life goes beyond confession and water baptism. It is about living victoriously, just as Jesus did when He died and rose again. Through baptism in the Holy Spirit, we receive the power to:

1. Produce spiritual fruit,
2. Sharpen our gifts,
3. Die to ourselves and our desires, and
4. Yield fully to the Spirit's leading.

As we strengthen, we diligently pursue our most significant promise—everlasting life. This is the blueprint. I don't know where you are in your Holy Spirit journey. But I know this: If you follow the Holy Spirit's blueprint, you will experience a transformed life—and those watching you will witness God's power at work. God's plan is for everyone to implement His blueprint:

1. Salvation,
2. Baptism with water,
3. Baptism with the Holy Spirit, and
4. Walking in His power.

To live a blessed life, activate the Holy Spirit in everything you do. Get the Holy Spirit hookup—don't live without Him! The only way to fully reach the purpose God has for you is to grow beyond salvation and walk in the power of the Holy Spirit.

Steps to a Blessed and Victorious Life

1. Acknowledge where you are. Are you a non-believer? Have you accepted Jesus as your personal Savior?
2. Become a believer. Accept Jesus as your Lord and Savior. Be baptized in water, allowing the Holy Spirit to take residence within you.

Thank you for allowing me to share some of my life experiences with you. Looking back at the time I felt too embarrassed to raise my hand to speak about the Holy Spirit and revisiting my life experiences especially in high school and college years, God was prompting me to know more about the Holy Spirit all along. I was running from the Holy Spirit then, but now, I am running toward Him fully understanding all that He offers for this victorious life. Like the saints said at the community choir day when I was a teenager, I can say He is the head of my life, and I thank God that I am saved, sanctified, filled with the Holy Spirit, and baptized with the mighty burning fire.

I pray that as you have read this book, apply what you have learned, and use the accompanying workbook, *The Blueprint: How the Holy Spirit Connection Can Change Your Life*, you will see how the Holy Spirit is changing your life and leading you to the path He has planned for you. This is the blueprint!

BONUS

Scan the QR Code to listen to the song *Holy Spirit*.

BIBLIOGRAPHY

1. Jerry F. Hutchins, M.A., M.DIV. 2005. *Understanding the Holy Spirit and the Full Gospel Baptist Church Fellowship 2nd Edition.* Conyers, GA: Jerry F. Hutchins Ministries.

2. Wilmington, H.L. 1981. *Wilmington's Guide to the Bible.* Tyndale House Publishers, Inc.

www.ingramcontent.com/pod-product-compliance
Lightning Source LLC
LaVergne TN
LVHW010919110826
845149LV00013B/2427

* 9 7 8 1 9 6 4 1 1 1 1 4 8 *